Number Skills

Math Projects and Activities for Grades K-3

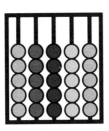

Written by Denise Bieniek

Illustrated by Paige Billin-Frye

10 9 8 7 6 5 4 3 2

Troll Early Learning Activities

Troll Early Learning Activities is a classroom-tested series designed to provide time-pressured teachers with a wide range of theme-related projects and activities to enhance lesson plans and enrich the curriculum. Each book focuses on a different area of early childhood learning, from math and writing to art and science. Using a wide range of activities, each title in this series is chockful of innovative ideas, handy reproducible pages, puzzles and games, classroom projects, suggestions for bulletin boards and learning centers, and much more.

With highly interactive student projects and teacher suggestions that make learning fun, Troll Early Learning Activities is an invaluable classroom resource you'll turn to again and again. We hope you will enjoy using the worksheets and activities presented in these books. And we know your students will benefit from the dynamic, creative learning environment you have created!

Titles in this series:

Animal Friends: Projects and Activities for Grades K-3

Circle Time Fun: Projects and Activities for Grades Pre-K-2

Classroom Decorations: Ideas for a Creative Classroom

Early Literacy Skills: Projects and Activities for Grades K-3

Helping Hands: Small Motor Skills Projects and Activities

Hi, Neighbor! Projects and Activities About Our Community

Number Skills: Math Projects and Activities for Grades K-3

People of the World: Multicultural Projects and Activities

Our World: Science Projects and Activities for Grades K-3

Seasons and Holidays: Celebrations All Year Long

Story Time: Skill-Building Projects and Activities for Grades K-3

Time, Money, Measurement: Projects and Activities Across the Curriculum

---

Metric Conversion Chart

1 inch = 2.54 cm	1 foot = .305 m	1 yard = .914 m
1 mile = 1.61 km	1 fluid ounce = 29.573 ml	1 cup = .24 l
1 pint = .473 l	1 teaspoon = 4.93 ml	1 tablespoon = 14.78 ml

Contents

Object Dominoes

Materials:

- crayons or markers
- scissors
- glue
- 3" x 5" index cards
- clear contact paper

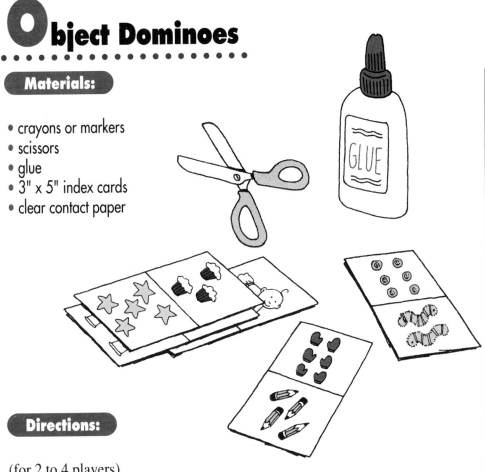

Directions:

(for 2 to 4 players)

1. Reproduce the art on page 6 twice. Color the figures and cut each group out.

2. Draw a line down the center of 36 3" x 5" white index cards. Then arrange two domino pictures on the front of each index card, facing away from the center, as shown (for example, one puppy on one half and five kites on the other half). Repeat for the remaining dominoes, creating various combinations.

3. Laminate the dominoes.

4. To play, place the dominoes facedown on the table. Ask each player to choose six dominoes and place them faceup in front of him- or herself.

5. The youngest player goes first and places a domino faceup in the middle of the playing surface. The next player then matches one end of one of his or her dominoes with one end of that first domino, making sure that the numbers of objects pictured in each half are the same. (The objects themselves may be different, such as two shoes and two telephones.) Play continues around the circle, with players matching up numbers of objects.

6. If a player does not have a domino that matches, he or she may draw one or two new dominoes from the facedown pile. If that player still does not have a match, the next player goes.

7. The first player who uses all of his or her dominoes in the game is the winner.

Object Dominoes

Baby Bird Number Match

- crayons or markers
- scissors
- oaktag
- glue
- clear contact paper
- folder with pocket
- Velcro

Directions:

1. Reproduce the art on page 8 eleven times. Color the figures and cut them out.

2. Mount the nests and birds onto oaktag and cut out again.

3. On each nest, write a number from zero to ten.

4. Laminate the front and back of each pattern.

5. To play, ask children to lay out the bird nests on a table or the floor. Then ask students to sit the same number of baby birds on the rim of each nest as is written on the nest.

6. Nests and baby birds may be stored in the pockets of the folder and left on the bookshelf for use during free time or book time.

7. To help students learn or review number recognition, write a number from zero to ten on 11 birds. Glue a piece of Velcro on the upper edge of each nest and on the lower edge of each bird. Ask students to match numbers that are the same. Then make a tree and hang it and the bird nests on a wall. Attach a bag or other pouch and store the birds in it.

8. You may also wish to use the birds and nest to review shape and colors with students. Glue a shape to each nest and bird and ask students to match the shapes. (Vary the sizes and types of each shape to promote greater understanding, e.g., a large equilateral triangle and a small right triangle.) Or color each nest and several birds matching colors. Then ask children to match same-colored nests and birds.

Baby Bird Number Match

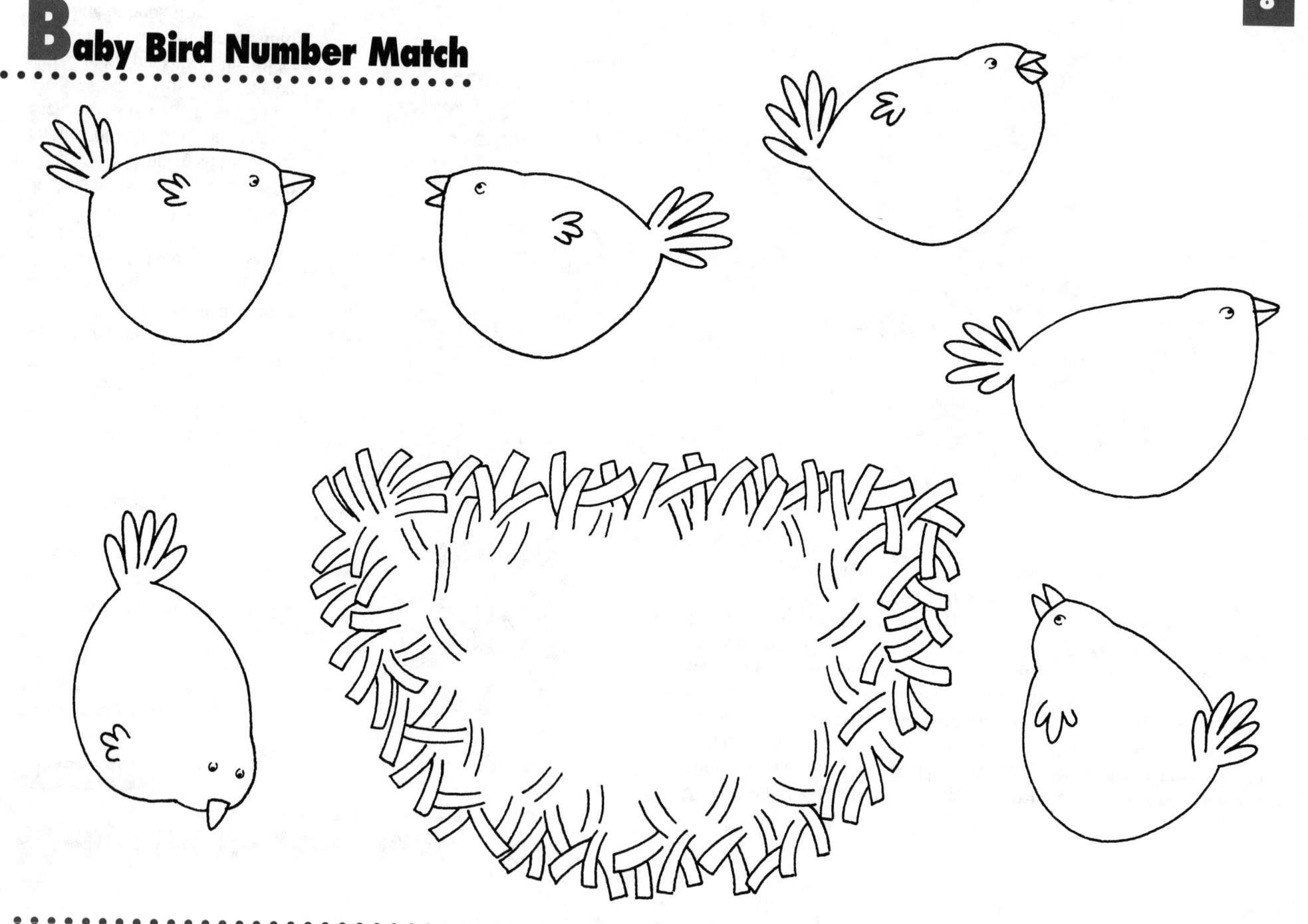

Bean Bag Toss

Materials:

- dry beans—all sizes and shapes
- clean, old socks (without holes)
- rubber bands
- scissors
- oaktag
- markers

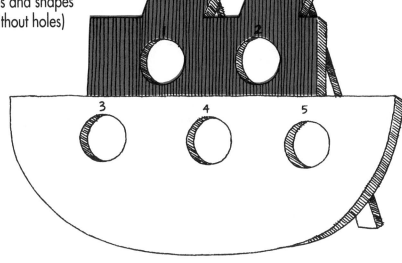

Directions:

1. Before making the bean bags, let children explore the dry beans. Place each type in a different container so students may feel them and compare their shapes, sizes, and the sounds they make when moved.

2. Pour enough beans into each sock to fill half the foot. Then twist the sock closed and wrap a rubber band tightly around the sock at the twist.

3. Cut off the remainder of the sock about 1" to 2" above the rubber band, as shown.

4. Use oaktag to make targets, such as:

A clown holding balloons—cut the center of the balloons out and label each with a different number score from one to five.

A ship with portholes—cut the center of the portholes out and label each with a different number score from one to five.

A lion tamer holding a hoop—cut the center from the hoop and label the hole with a number score.

5. Students—individually or in small groups—may toss their bean bags at the targets. Whoever gets the highest score after three tosses is the winner.

Name _____

Toy Store Magic •••••••••••••••••

Merlin the Magician has made all the colors in this toy store disappear. Use the code below to color in the picture.

1 = red   2 = blue   3 = yellow   4 = green   5 = orange
6 = purple   7 = brown   8 = pink   9 = black   10 = gray

Number Wheel Fun

Materials:

- crayons or markers
- oaktag
- scissors
- old magazines and workbooks
- glue
- clothespins (that open and shut)

Directions:

1. Draw a circle 10" in diameter on oaktag and cut out.

2. Divide the circle into eight sections, as shown.

3. In each section, write a number that the class is learning or reviewing. Then draw or cut out pictures from old magazines and glue them onto each section, matching the number of objects to the number written in the section. (Be sure to cover the written number in each section with the pictures.)

4. Write a number on one side of a clothespin that matches one of those written in a section of the oaktag circle. Repeat until there is one clothespin for each section of the number circle.

5. To play, ask children to match each numbered clothespin to the section with the same number of objects by pinning the clothespin to the correct section.

6. As children become more adept at the game, ask them to create number wheels of their own to share with classmates.

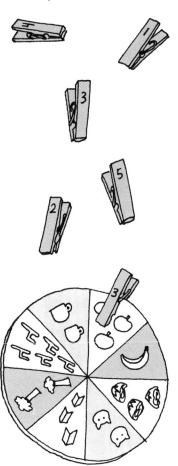

Button Sort

Materials:

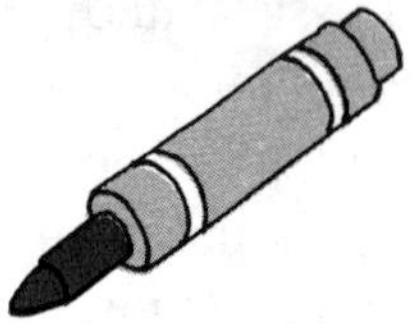

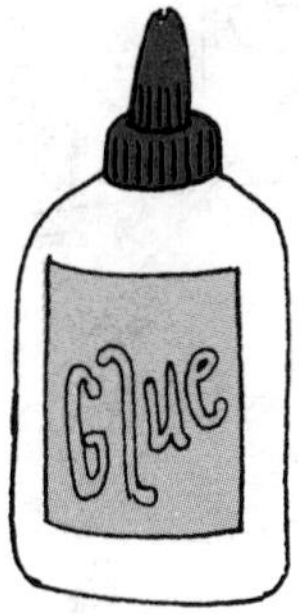

- crayons or markers
- scissors
- oaktag
- glue
- buttons
- clothesline
- clothespins

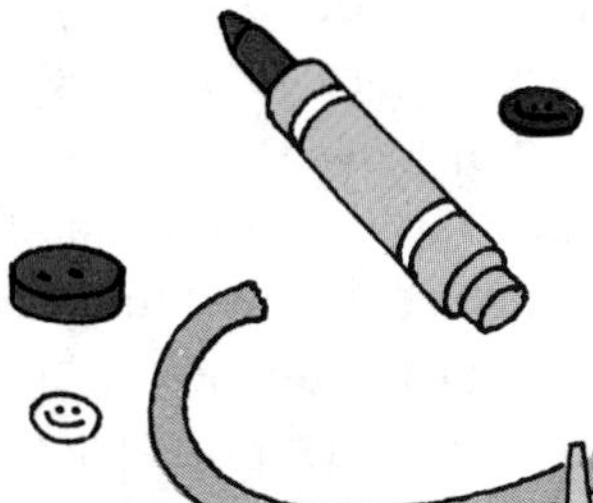

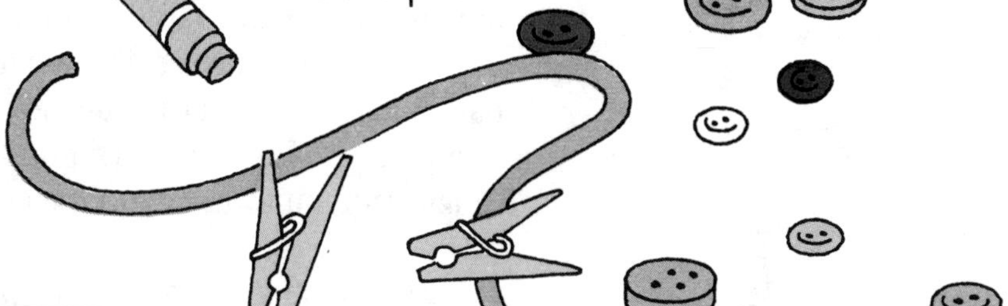

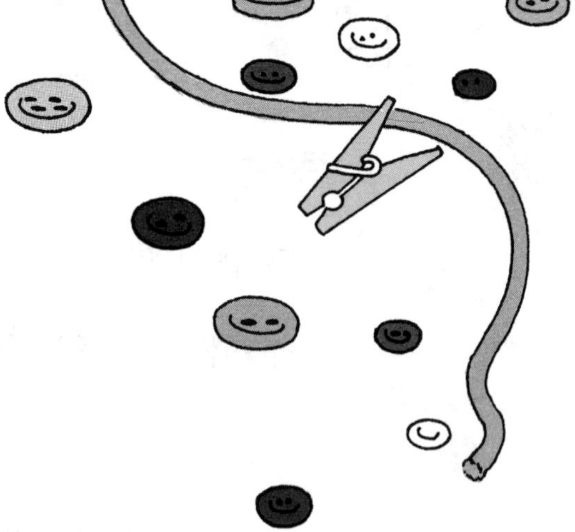

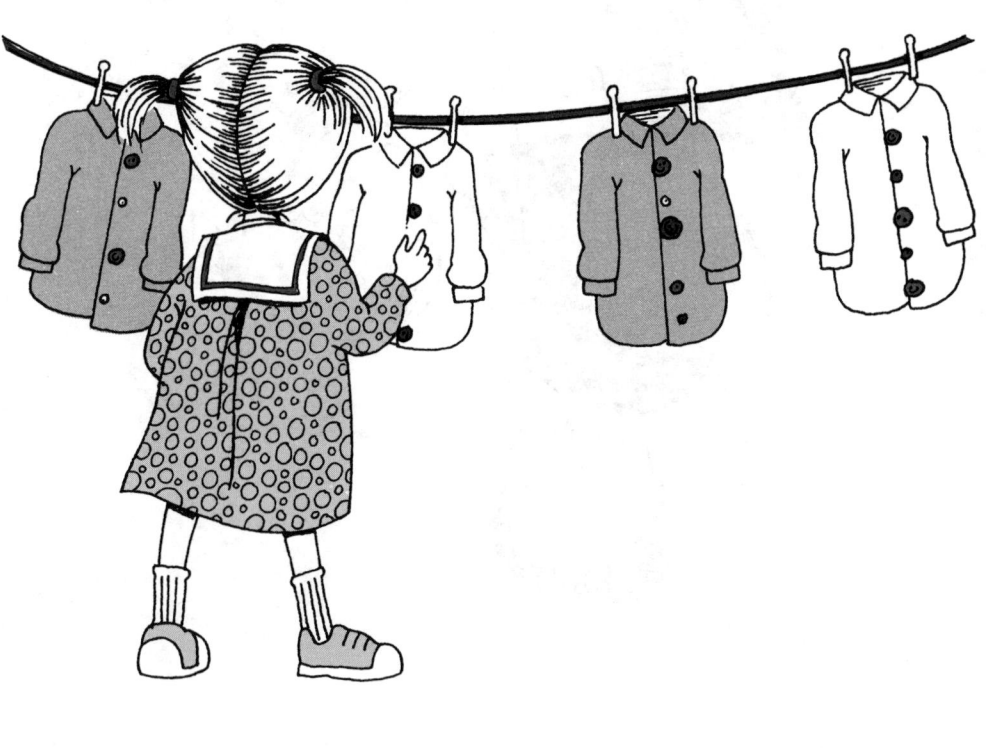

Directions:

1. Divide the class into small groups. Set out a collection of assorted buttons for each group. Encourage students to explore the buttons, commenting on size, shape, color, and number of holes.

2. Ask children to work together to sort the buttons according to the number of holes in each type.

3. Reproduce the art on page 13 once for each child. Have children color the shirts, mount them on oaktag, and cut them out.

4. Ask students to glue buttons on their shirts, choosing buttons in one of several different ways. Some suggestions are:

Whatever buttons they choose

Buttons whose combined number of holes will equal a specific amount

Buttons with a specific number of holes

5. Set up a clothesline in the room at students' height. Help children arrange their shirts on the clothesline in serial order (from least to most buttons), or let them make patterns with their shirts (for example, one hole-two holes-one hole-two holes).

#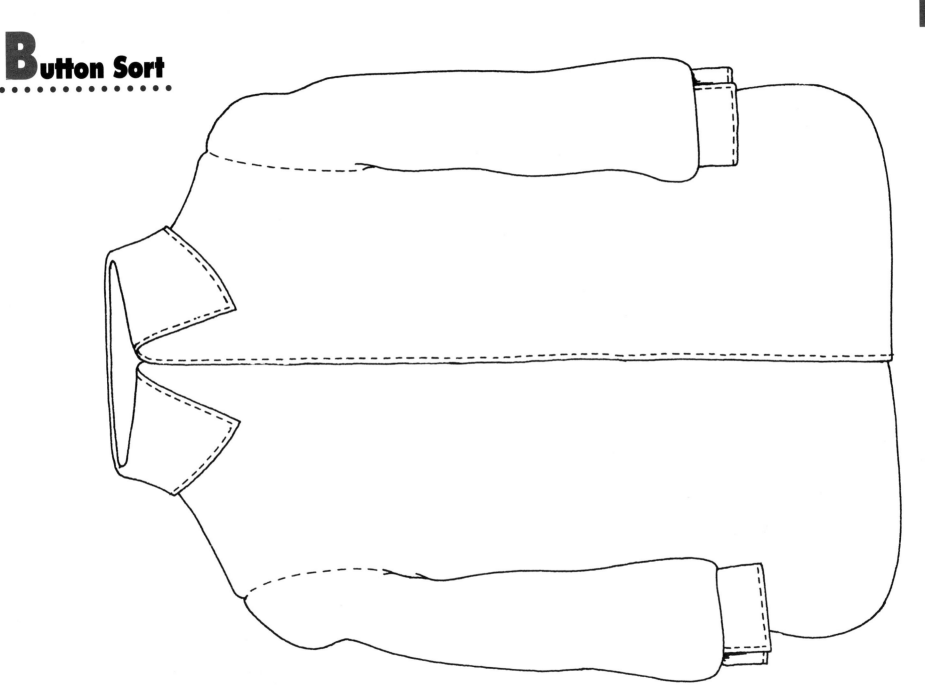

Button Sort

Ordinal Ocean Fishing Game

Materials:

- crayons or markers
- scissors
- hole puncher
- paper clips
- blue or green construction paper or large sheet of butcher paper painted blue or green
- rulers
- yarn
- magnets

Directions:

1. Reproduce the art on page 15 one or more times. Color the sea creatures and cut them out.

2. Punch a hole in the mouth of each sea creature and fasten a paper clip in it. On each animal, write an ordinal number from one to ten (or greater, depending on students' abilities). For example, *tenth* may be written as "tenth" or "10th."

3. Lay blue or green construction paper on the floor so it resembles a pond. (Or cut a large sheet of butcher paper and paint it blue or green with the class.) Scatter the sea creatures in the pond.

4. To make each fishing rod, tie one end of an 18" length of yarn to a ruler and the other end to a magnet.

5. Let two children at a time play the game. Have children use their fishing rods to "catch" the sea creatures with the magnets (which will attract the paper clips).

6. After all the sea creatures have been caught, ask children to put them in order from smallest ordinal number to largest. If possible, leave the game in a corner of the classroom for students to play individually or in pairs during free time.

Ordinal Ocean Fishing Game

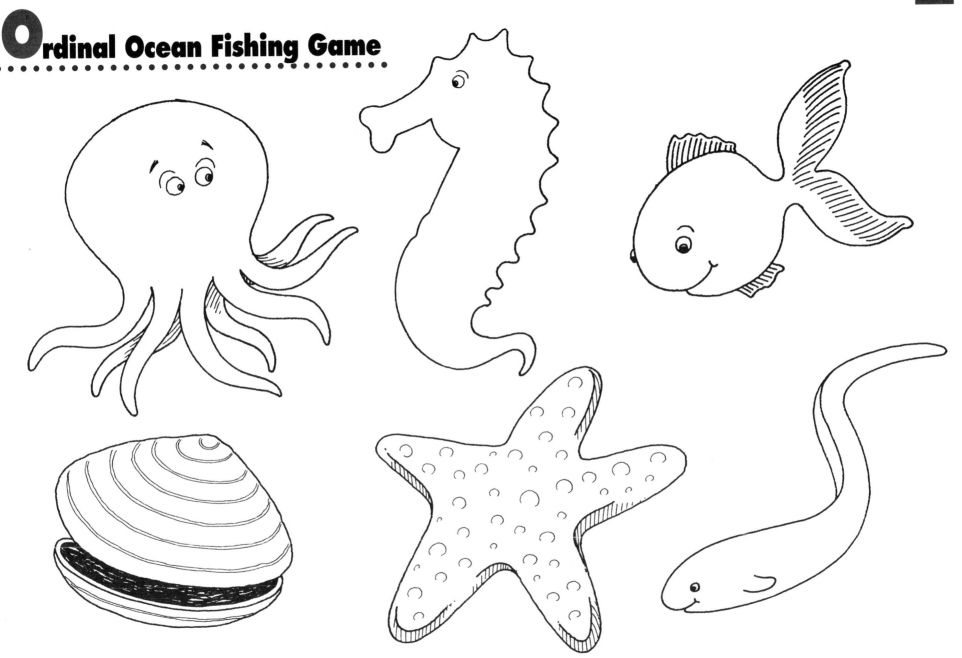

Math Sentence Clothesline

Materials:

- crayons or markers
- clothespins (that open and shut)
- scissors
- clothesline

Directions:

1. Reproduce the art on page 17 several times. Color the patterns and cut them out.

2. On each piece of clothing, write a number from zero to ten, or a math symbol (for example, an equal sign, or the sign for greater than, less than, addition, subtraction, division, or multiplication).

3. Hang a clothesline across an easily accessible space in the classroom, at students' height. Attach a few clothespins to the line.

4. To play, gather the class or a small group in front of the clothesline. Attach the first number, an addition symbol, another number, and the equal sign to the clothesline, in order. Ask a student to come up to the line and tell what the answer to the equation is.

5. Repeat, using other addends. Then vary the game by leaving one of the addends blank and including the sum.

6. To create an introduction or review of the concepts of "greater than" and "less than," use the number clothes with the greater than and less than symbols. Place one number on the clothesline and add the greater than symbol next to it. Leave the last space blank for a student to fill in.

7. When the students are familiar with the activity, ask them to create math equations for their classmates to solve.

Math Sentence Clothesline

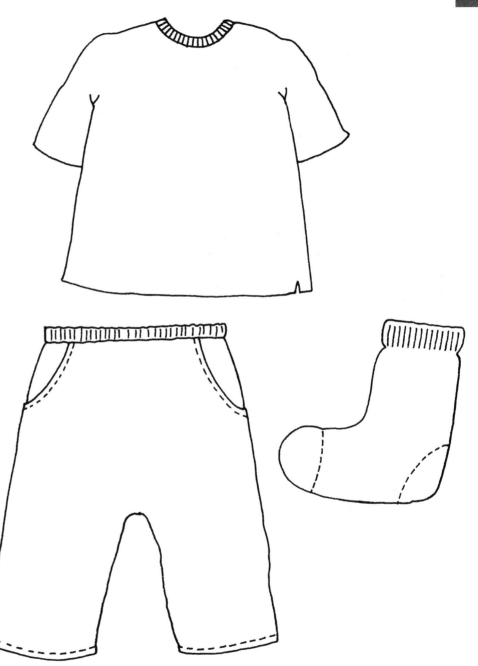

Five Little Monkey Puppets

Materials:

- crayons or markers
- scissors
- oaktag
- glue
- craft sticks

Directions:

1. Reproduce the art on page 19 two times, and the art on pages 20 and 21 once. Color the figures and props, mount them on oaktag, and cut them out.

2. Glue a craft stick to the bottom of each monkey and prop, as shown.

3. Use the cutouts to act out the following chant.

> Five little monkeys jumping on the bed.
> One fell down and bumped his head.
> Mommy called the doctor, and the doctor said,
> "Keep those monkeys off the bed!"
>
> Four little monkeys jumping on the bed . . .

4. Continue the chant with one fewer monkey each verse. After each verse, ask the students how many monkeys are left on the bed. Point out that at first there were five; if one fell off, that leaves four on the bed, and so on.

5. When the chant is finished, ask the class some questions about what happened in the story. Some suggestions are:

> Do you think those monkeys are allowed to jump on their bed? Are you allowed to jump on your bed?
>
> How do you think those monkeys felt when they fell off the bed?
>
> If you were one of those monkeys, would you listen to the doctor, or would you jump on the bed again?
>
> What do you think happened when all the monkeys finally fell off the bed?

6. Ask each child to write a story and draw pictures about something else the five mischievous monkeys like to do. Leave the props out for students to use during free time.

Five Little Monkey Puppets

Five Little Monkey Puppets

Five Little Monkey Puppets

Base-Ten Addition

Use base-ten squares on page 24 and a place-value chart to answer the problems below.

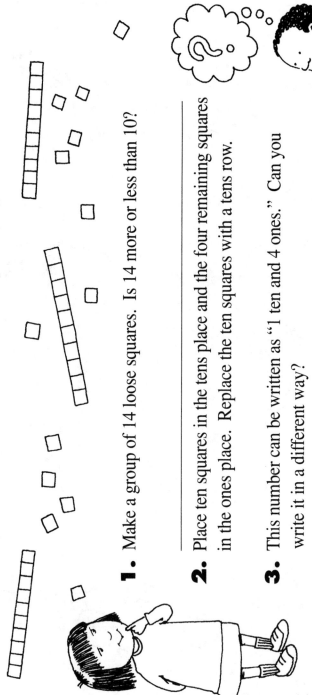

1. Make a group of 14 loose squares. Is 14 more or less than 10?

2. Place ten squares in the tens place and the four remaining squares in the ones place. Replace the ten squares with a tens row.

3. This number can be written as "1 ten and 4 ones." Can you write it in a different way?

4. Next, make a group of 19 loose squares. Group the squares on the place-value chart. Replace one of the groups with a tens row. Now write this number three different ways.

_____

_____

5. Show the number 47 using the tens rows and ones squares.

6. Show the solution to this equation, using the tens rows and ones squares: 35 + 6.

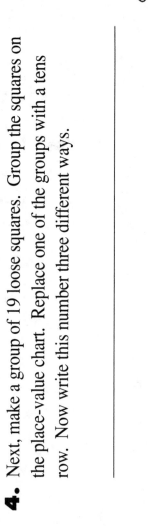

Base-Ten Subtraction

Use base-ten squares on page 24 and a place-value chart to answer the problems below.

1. Make a group of 7 loose squares. Is 7 more or less than 10?

_____

2. Place the 7 squares in the ones place and a tens row in the tens place. What number is this?

_____

3. Remove four squares from this number. What is the new number?

_____

Write the number in three different ways.

_____

4. Show the problem 63 − 8 using the tens rows and ones squares. What is the answer?

_____

5. Show the problem 77 − 21 using the tens rows and the ones squares. Write the answer in three different ways.

_____

6. Show the number 143 on the place-value chart.

Base-Ten Squares

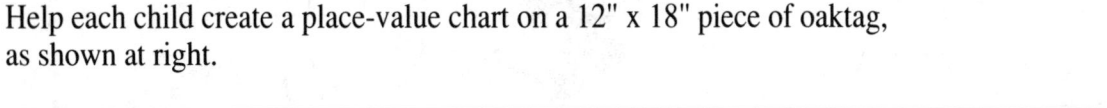

Reproduce this page twice for each student. Have children cut ten rows into rows of ten, and two rows into single squares.

Help each child create a place-value chart on a 12" x 18" piece of oaktag, as shown at right.

Hundreds | Tens | Ones

Hundreds Chart Ideas

1. Reproduce the hundreds chart on page 26 once for each child.

2. Encourage students to describe any patterns they see in the chart. Some possible patterns are:

Counting by twos skips every other number.

In each column, the numbers in the tens places change while the number in the ones places stays the same.

The last column is a tens sequence.

The numbers increase by 11 from the top left corner to the lower right corner.

The numbers increase by 9 from the top right corner to the lower left corner.

3. The hundreds chart is a good way to review multiples. Have students cross out all the multiples of 2, 3, 4, or other numbers. Before students can cross out a number, they must tell how it is a multiple of the number chosen. For example, if multiples of 3 are being crossed out, a child may say, "Nine can be crossed out because 3 x 3 = 9."

4. You may also wish to review even and odd numbers using the hundreds chart. Point out that crossing out all even numbers skips every other number, and the same is true when all odd numbers are crossed out.

5. For older students, consider using the chart to discuss prime numbers. Explain what the definition of a prime number is; it has only two different factors, 1 and the number itself. Then work together as a class to find all the prime numbers on the hundreds chart.

Name _____

Hundreds Chart

1	2	3	4	5	6	7	8	9	10
11	12	13	14	15	16	17	18	19	20
21	22	23	24	25	26	27	28	29	30
31	32	33	34	35	36	37	38	39	40
41	42	43	44	45	46	47	48	49	50
51	52	53	54	55	56	57	58	59	60
61	62	63	64	65	66	67	68	69	70
71	72	73	74	75	76	77	78	79	80
81	82	83	84	85	86	87	88	89	90
91	92	93	94	95	96	97	98	99	100

Flowerpot Math

- crayons or markers
- scissors
- craft sticks
- glue
- plastic cups
- construction paper
- dough or modeling clay

Directions:

1. Reproduce the flower tops on page 28 once for each child. Have children color the flowers and cut them out.

2. Have each student glue a craft stick to the back of each flower, leaving most of the stick free. Children may also wish to color the craft sticks to resemble stems.

3. Show children how to cover plastic cups with construction paper. Then put a ball of dough or modeling clay in the bottom of each child's cup, filling it halfway.

4. Use the flowers and pots to illustrate the concepts of "greater than" and "less than." Have each child pair up with a classmate. Instruct students to place four flowers in one cup and two in the other. Ask the students to tell which flowerpot has more flowers and which has less.

5. Advance to less noticeable differences between the two amounts. Then ask students to create their own "more than" and "less than" equations.

6. Use the flowers and pots to learn about number conservation. Ask students to place six flowers in their pots. Compare and contrast the different ways students arranged their flowers, emphasizing that all the pots contain six flowers. Continue with other numbers of flowers.

7. Make a set for the classroom math center. Write a number from 0 to 10 on each flowerpot and in the middle of each flower. Students can match flowers to flower pots with the same numbers written on them. Or leave the flowers blank and have students count out the appropriate number of flowers for each numbered cup. (You will need more than eight flowers per child for this activity!)

Going Shopping

Materials:

- crayons or markers
- scissors
- 3" x 5" index cards
- tape
- folder with pocket

Directions:

1. Reproduce the art on pages 30 and 31 once. Color the patterns and cut them out.

2. Cut 3" x 5" index cards in half and create price tags for the items for sale. Use money symbols, such as cents and dollar signs, where applicable.

3. Tape the cash register on the chalkboard or a classroom wall. In the blank window of the cash register, tape half of an index card with a price total written on it. Ask a student to read the amount using money vocabulary (i.e., cents, dollars).

4. Tape the items for sale around the register. Ask a pair of students to choose items that will equal the total shown on the register. Then add up the prices of the items to check whether they match the total on the register.

5. When children are familiar with the activity, choose one child to be the cashier, who will add up the items, and another to be the customer, who will choose the items. The customer should try to choose items whose total will match the total on the register. After the cashier has checked to make sure the addition is correct, he or she must give the customer a receipt for the sale. If the amounts do not match, the customer must try again.

6. Store this activity in a folder with pockets. Place the folder in the math center for children to use during free time.

Going Shopping

Name _____

Connect the Dots

Connect the even-numbered dots in order. Then connect the odd-numbered dots in order. Now color the picture!

Halves Activity Folder

Materials:

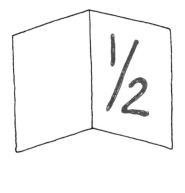

- crayons or markers
- scissors
- 5" x 7" index cards
- glue
- large sheet of oaktag

Directions:

1. Reproduce the patterns on pages 34 and 35. Color the pictures and cut them out.

2. Fold twelve 5" x 7" index cards in half. Glue one picture to the front of each index card, as shown.

3. Using a marker, draw a line across each picture. Draw some of the lines right down the middle and some lines off to the left or the right.

4. On the inside of each picture card divided exactly down the middle, write the fraction for one-half (1/2). Leave the insides of the picture cards divided unevenly blank.

5. Fold a large piece of oaktag in half. Glue six picture cards on the left and six pictures on the right of the inside of the oaktag folder, as shown. Write "1/2" on the front cover.

6. Read the title with the class, then open the oaktag folder. Point to one picture card and ask the class if the picture was divided in half or not. To check the answer, open the card.

7. Leave the folder in the math center for children to play with during free time.

Halves Activity Folder

Halves Activity Folder

Don't Be Late!

Materials:

- crayons or markers
- scissors
- glue
- small and large pieces of oaktag
- Velcro
- clear plastic bag
- stapler

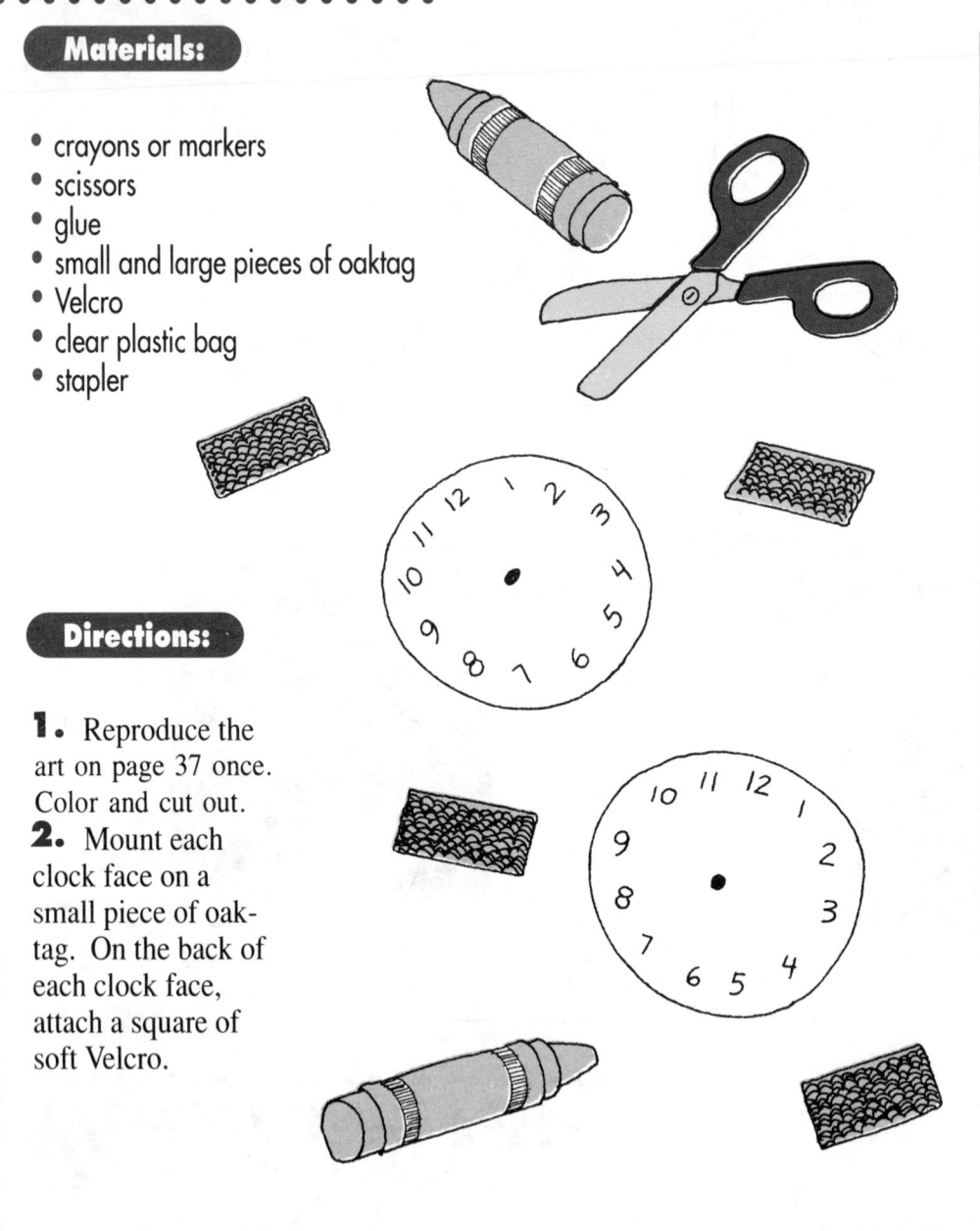

Directions:

1. Reproduce the art on page 37 once. Color and cut out.

2. Mount each clock face on a small piece of oak-tag. On the back of each clock face, attach a square of soft Velcro.

3. On a large piece of oaktag, write a short story that incorporates the use of different times. For example:

Peter's Journal

July 15

   I woke up at 8:30 a.m. It was a sunny day, so we went to the beach. We got to the beach at 10:00 a.m. and I went swimming in the ocean. I found some beautiful shells when I went walking on the sand!

   We ate lunch at 12:30 p.m. I had a peanut butter sandwich and apple juice with two cookies for dessert. Mom told me to wait until 2:00 p.m. to go swimming again so I wouldn't get a stomach cramp.

   At 4:00 p.m., we went home. It felt like a million pounds of sand was stuck in my bathing suit!

   We went to a barbecue at Uncle John's and Aunt Michelle's house at 6:15 p.m. There was so much food that I didn't know what to choose. Finally, I had a little of everything. It was delicious!

   At 9:00 p.m., I went to bed. I was so tired that I couldn't even finish writing in my journal.

---

4. Leave a space next to each place in the story where a time is mentioned. Stick a square of hard Velcro in these spaces.

5. Draw hands on each clock face to match one of the times mentioned in the story. Staple a clear plastic bag to the bottom of the large piece of oaktag and place the clock faces inside.

6. Read the story aloud to the class. Ask a volunteer to place the clock that matches each time in the appropriate space.

Don't Be Late!

Palindrome Pals

Otto and Anna are palindrome pals. A palindrome is a word that is spelled the same forward and backward.

Numbers can also be palindromes. Look at each of the equations below. Figure out what the missing palindrome is. Now make up some palindromes of your own!

$$
\begin{array}{r}
242 \\
+\ 353 \\
\hline
\end{array}
$$

$$
\begin{array}{r}
939 \\
-\ 717 \\
\hline
\end{array}
$$

$$
\begin{array}{r}
1001 \\
+2002 \\
\hline
\end{array}
$$

$$
\begin{array}{r}
535 \\
-\ 333 \\
\hline
\end{array}
$$

$$
\begin{array}{r}
6556 \\
+2222 \\
\hline
\end{array}
$$

Cross-Number Puzzle

· ·

The figure below looks like a crossword puzzle, but it's really a cross-number puzzle! Solve each equation or question and write the answer in the appropriate space.

Across

B. 816 + 816
C. Prime number between 11 and 17
D. 7,893 - 1,000
F. 4,040 + 3,030
G. 853 - 111
I. 500 + 405
K. 3700 - 99

Down

A. 20,000 + 31,630
C. 1,620 + 100
D. 27 + 33
E. 547 - 230
H. Palindrome for 4,664
J. 250 + 250
L. Palindrome for 111

Super Math Bingo

23 – 10

13

13

13

1. Reproduce the bingo game board on page 41 once for each child. Write numbers from 1 to 25 (or 1 to 100, depending on students' abilities) randomly on each game board.

2. Ask each child to cut out 25 squares of colored construction paper to fit over the spaces on his or her game board.

3. Tell the class that they will be playing a bingo math game. Call out simple addition and subtraction problems that students should be able to solve without pencil and paper (for example, "23 – 10"). Write each math sentence on the chalkboard to keep track of what numbers have been called.

4. If a child has the number that is the solution to a problem on his or her game board, that child may cover the number with a colored square of paper.

5. Vary each game by making the goal to cover up a row, a diagonal, the perimeter of the board, or the entire board. The winner is the first player to cover up the appropriate squares on his or her board.

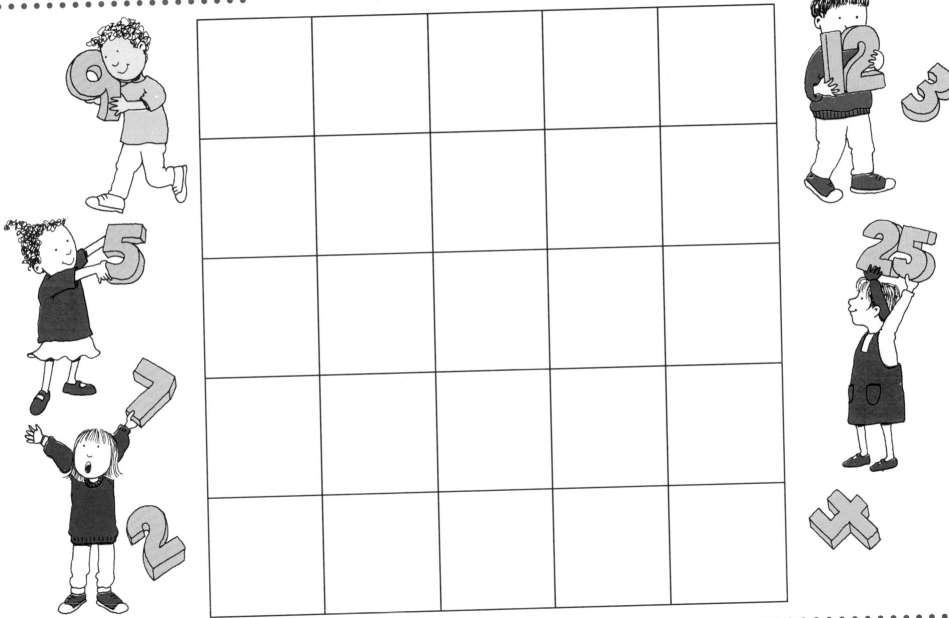

Super Math Bingo

Name _____

Messy Room • • • • • • • • • •

John and Jessie have to clean up their room. Help them figure out how many of each item they have to put away.

1. How many more books are there than stuffed animals? _____

2. Are there more cassette tapes or shoes? _____

3. Add together the cars and trucks and the stuffed animals. What is the total? _____

4. Are there fewer stuffed animals or shoes? _____

5. How many more cars and trucks are there than shoes? _____

Bonus work: On a separate piece of paper, make a chart showing the things you have in your room at home. How many of each item is there?

Clothing Graph

1. To help children learn or review graphing skills, make a class graph about students' clothing. Ask volunteers to suggest categories (such as colors, patterns, articles of clothing, and so on) for the graph. Write students' suggestions on a chart on the chalkboard, as shown.

2. Proceed in one of two ways. You may wish to discuss each student's clothing individually. For example, volunteers may say, "Bobby has a red striped shirt and blue pants." You would then put tally marks under a red column, a blue column, and a stripe column.

3. You may instead choose to have students raise their hands as you call out each category. Ask a volunteer to count the hands each time, then write the total in the appropriate place on the chalkboard.

4. Use the chart to make a bar graph with the children on a large piece of oaktag. Give students different-colored markers to use to fill in each part of the graph.

5. Discuss how the graph represents the different types of clothing worn. If desired, entitle the graph "Our Clothing" and attach it to a wall in the math center for all to see.

Name _____

Candy Count
· · · · · · · · · ·

Beth and Billy want to buy as much candy as they can at the store. They each have 50 cents. Write down some of the choices Beth and Billy can make.

LOLLIPOPS
3 for 15¢

PEPPERMINT
STICKS
5¢

LICORICE
20¢

CHOCOLATE
DROPS
10¢

CANDY BARS
40¢

2¢
GUMBALLS

Candy

Billy

Beth

TOTAL COST: _____

TOTAL COST: _____

TOTAL COST: _____

Name _____

Time Will Tell

Guess how long it will take you to do each of the things listed below. Write your guesses on the lines provided. Then ask a friend to use a clock or watch with a second hand to time how long each task actually takes. Remember, it's not a race—so take your time!

	Guess	**Actual Time**
clap your hands 20 times		
do 15 jumping jacks		
write the entire alphabet		
write your full name		
do six somersaults		
sing your favorite song		
eat a cookie		
drink a glass of water		

Best Books About Math

Read some or all of the following books involving various math concepts. Place the books in the reading center for students to review during free time.

Anno's Math Games by Anno (Putnam, 1987)

What Comes in 2's, 3's, and 4's? by Suzanne Aker (Simon and Schuster, 1990)

Charts & Graphs by Caroline Arnold (Franklin Watts, 1984)

Measurements by Caroline Arnold (Franklin Watts, 1984)

Numbers by Philip Carona (Childrens Press, 1982)

Count Your Way Through Japan by Jim Haskins (Carolrhoda, 1987)

Arthur's Funny Money by Lillian Hoban (HarperCollins, 1980)

How Much Is a Million? by David M. Schwartz (Lothrop Lee, 1985)

Zero Is Not Nothing by Harry Sitomer and Mindel Sitomer (HarperCollins, 1978)

Solomon Grundy, Born on Oneday: A Finite Arithmetic Puzzle by Malcolm E. Weiss (HarperCollins, 1977)

Time by Feenie Ziner and Elizabeth Thompson (Childrens Press, 1982)

Thermometer Readings

1. A good way to point out to students how math is used in everyday life is to chart the temperature. Begin with a basic discussion of thermometers to determine how much the children know about temperature. Show students a thermometer and explain how it measures the temperature. (The mercury expands as it gets warmer and is forced up the tube of the thermometer; it contracts in the cold and moves down the tube.) For older children, you may also wish to discuss the mathematical difference between Fahrenheit and Celsius. (The Fahrenheit scale uses 32° as the freezing point of water and 212° as its boiling point; the Celsius scale uses 0° as the freezing point of water and 100° for its boiling point.)

2. Ask volunteers to guess what the temperature is outside. Write students' guesses on the chalkboard. Then check the actual temperature on an outdoor thermometer to see how accurate the guesses were.

3. Discuss the range of temperatures for each season in your geographic area. Using a map, show students where colder and warmer climates are located in relation to where they live.

4. Reproduce the monthly weather chart on page 48 once for each student. Ask students to fill in the days for the upcoming month. At the beginning of each day, ask a volunteer to read the temperature on the outdoor thermometer. Have students record the temperature on their weather charts. (You may also wish to have students record the type of weather for each day, such as ''sunny,'' ''windy,'' and so on.)

5. At the end of the month, have the class work together to create a bar graph showing the various temperatures for the month.

6. Create math problems geared to students' abilities based on the temperature chart. For example, ask which week had the highest temperatures and which week had the lowest. For older students, introduce the concept of averaging by adding together the temperatures for a week and dividing to find out the mean temperature.

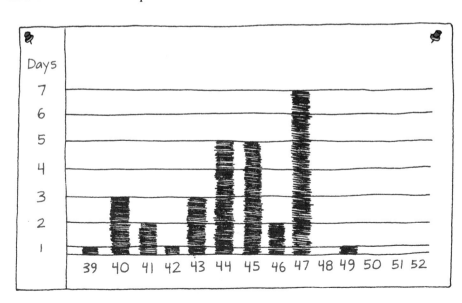

Name _____

Thermometer Thoughts

Fill in the month and days on the calendar below. Each day, record the temperature in the appropriate space.

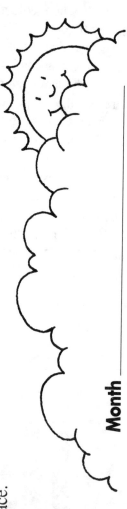

Month _____

Sun	Mon	Tues	Wed	Thurs	Fri	Sat

What's the Temperature?

Look at each of the thermometers below. Write the temperature shown on each thermometer in Fahrenheit and Celsius on the lines provided.

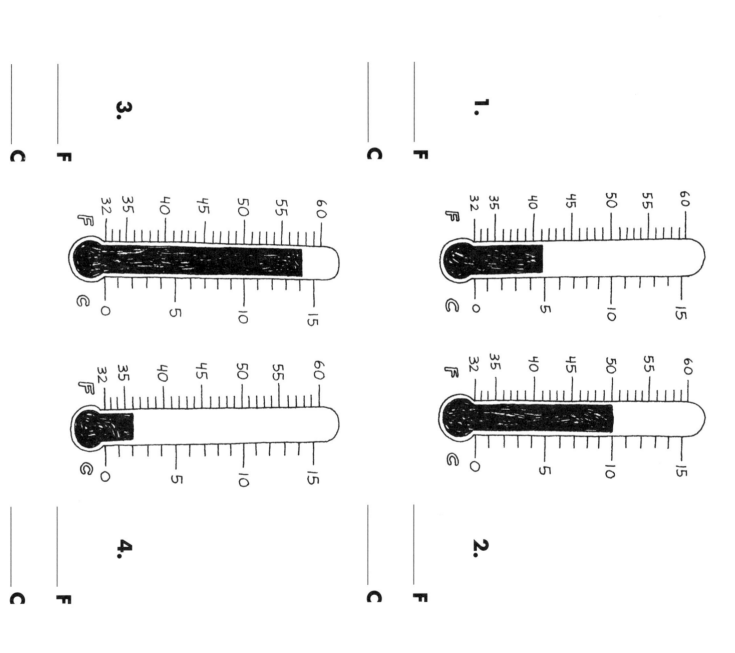

1.

F _____

C _____

2.

F _____

C _____

3.

F _____

C _____

4.

F _____

C _____

Name _____

It's Magic!

Each row and diagonal adds up to the same number in each magic square below. Fill in the missing numbers to make the magic squares work. Don't forget to say "Abracadabra!"

		9
	3	5
	4	9

4		9
2	6	4

Now see if you can make one of your own!

		9
	8	
10	7	7

Super Chefs

Cooking is an excellent way to help children learn about measurement and fractions. Have the class work in small groups to make batches of the following recipe for blueberry muffins. Supervise each group to ensure that the proper amounts of each ingredient are used.

Materials:

- 1 cup flour
- 1/2 cup wheat germ
- 1/4 cup sugar
- 2 teaspoons baking powder
- 1/4 teaspoon salt
- 1/4 cup vegetable oil
- 3/4 cup skim milk

- 1 cup blueberries
- 1 egg
- mixing bowls
- wooden spoons
- paper muffin liners
- muffin tins

Yield: Approximately 8–10 muffins

Directions:

1. Mix together the flour, wheat germ, sugar, salt, and baking powder in a large mixing bowl.

2. Place the milk and the vegetable oil in another mixing bowl.

3. Add the egg to the milk and vegetable oil and mix.

4. Make an indentation in the middle of the dry mixture. Then pour the milk, vegetable oil, and egg in the center and stir until everything is mixed together. (Do not stir until the mixture is smooth; it should remain slightly lumpy.)

5. Gradually stir in the blueberries.

6. Preheat the oven to 400°F. Place the muffin liners inside the muffin tins.

7. Fill each muffin liner approximately 2/3 full.

8. Place the muffin tins in the oven. Bake at 400°F for 22-25 minutes. To test for doneness, insert a toothpick in a muffin. If it comes out clean, the muffins are done. If batter sticks to the toothpick, continue baking for two more minutes.

Name _____

Recipe Races
• • • • • • • • • • • • •

Betsy the baker has written down the ingredients for a chocolate-chip cookie recipe. Show Betsy a faster way to write out each amount. The first ingredient has been done for you.

two and one-quarter cups of flour   2 1/4 c. flour

one cup of sugar   _____

one-half cup of brown sugar   _____

one teaspoon of baking soda   _____

one-half teaspoon of salt   _____

one cup of butter   _____

two eggs   _____

one teaspoon of vanilla   _____

two and one-half cups of chocolate chips   _____

three-quarters cup of walnuts   _____

Mathletes Day

Arrange for a class "Mathletes Day" with various math contests and games. If desired, invite other classes to join in the fun. Begin by discussing the celebration with the class. Ask if anyone has suggestions for different events. Some suggestions are:

Math Bee—Divide the class into two groups. Play a game similar to a spelling bee, but using math problems. If a student answers a problem incorrectly, he or she is out of the game. Then the next student must try to answer the same problem correctly. Continue playing until there is one student left in each group. Have these two students take turns solving more problems until there is a winner.

Even-and-Odd Leapfrog—Set up two winding paths of construction-paper lily pads around the classroom. Tape the lily pads to the floor. Write even numbers on one path, and odd numbers on the other path. Divide the class into two teams, "Even" and "Odd." Each member of a team must leapfrog down the appropriate path to the end. Once a member has reached the end of the path, the next player may begin leapfrogging. The first team whose members complete the path is the winner.

Educated Guessers—Fill a jar with jellybeans, hard candy, or some other edible and countable item. Ask each child to guess how many of the item are in the jar. Have students write their guesses on scraps of paper with their names. After everyone has made a guess, empty the jar and count the items. The child whose guess is closest to the actual amount is the winner. Distribute the candy when the game is over.

If desired, invite parents and school workers to some of the events. You may also wish to make the muffin recipe on page 51 to serve with juice as refreshments for participants and guests.

Name _____

Square Off

Play the game below with a friend. Each player takes a turn by connecting any two dots next to each other with a line. If a player draws a line that completes a square, he or she may write the initial of his or her name in that square. Then the player may take another turn.

The player with the most squares at the end of the game is the winner!

Medical Math

1. Teaching children how to take their pulses not only helps them learn more about their health, but is a good way to reinforce addition and multiplication skills. Begin by helping each child locate his or her pulse on the wrist.

2. After children are comfortable finding their pulses, have them count how many times their hearts beat in a minute. Then have children count their pulse rates for 15 seconds. Help each child multiply that figure by 4 to get the total for 1 minute. Explain that 15 seconds four times equals 60 seconds, or 1 minute.

3. Tell children to line up next to each other. Have the first child on one end touch the child next to him or her. Then have that child touch the next child in line, and so on until the line is completed. Time how long the process takes from the first child to the last. Then divide that number by the number of children in the line. The result is the average time it takes for a nerve impulse to travel from a nerve ending to the brain, and then from the brain to a muscle.

4. Share some fun and interesting medical math facts with the class:

- The average human being's heart beats over 100,000 times a day.
- Your blood probably travels about 200 miles a day through your body.
- The average person has approximately 100,000 hairs on his or her head.
- Your fingernails grow about 2 inches each year.

Name

Binary Tricks

Here's a math trick that will amaze your friends!

Cut out each of the squares below. Then ask a friend to pick a number between 1 and 31. Lay the squares out in front of the friend and ask him or her to point to the squares that have the chosen number in them. Then add together the first numbers (in the upper left corner) of the chosen squares. The total will be the number your friend selected!

21

1 + 4 + 16

1	3	5	7
9	11	13	15
17	19	21	23
25	27	29	31

2	3	4	6
10	11	14	15
18	19	22	23
26	27	30	31

4	5	6	7
12	13	14	15
20	21	22	23
28	29	30	31

8	9	10	11
12	13	14	15
24	25	26	27
28	29	30	31

16	17	18	19
20	21	22	23
24	25	26	27
28	29	30	31

Unusual Measurements

1. When introducing or practicing measurement with a ruler, encourage children to use other, nonstandard types of measurement as well. For example, you may wish to ask each child to find out how many of his or her footprints are needed to measure the length of the classroom. Have students share their results with the class, and discuss why some answers are different from others.

2. Have students use more than one nonstandard unit of measurement to measure an object. For example, ask a student to measure the width of his or her desk using paper clips, then crayons.

3. Ask children to try to imagine what it would be like to use a nonstandard form of measurement all the time. Tell students to make up silly math problems involving nonstandard measurements. Have each student exchange his or her silly problems with a classmate and try to solve each other's problems.

What's My Rule?

1. Introduce or review the concept of Venn diagrams and sets with this activity. Begin by drawing a circle on the chalkboard.

2. Choose sets of something in the classroom familiar to students. For example, you might write about sets of toys in this way:

3. Ask children to think of the rule for the toys inside the circle (in the example, "Toys with Wheels"). Write the rule below the diagram.

4. Have volunteers help think of new sets for "What's My Rule?" After children are comfortable with this concept, draw overlapping circles to show two sets with a common subset. For example, you might describe bears in this way:

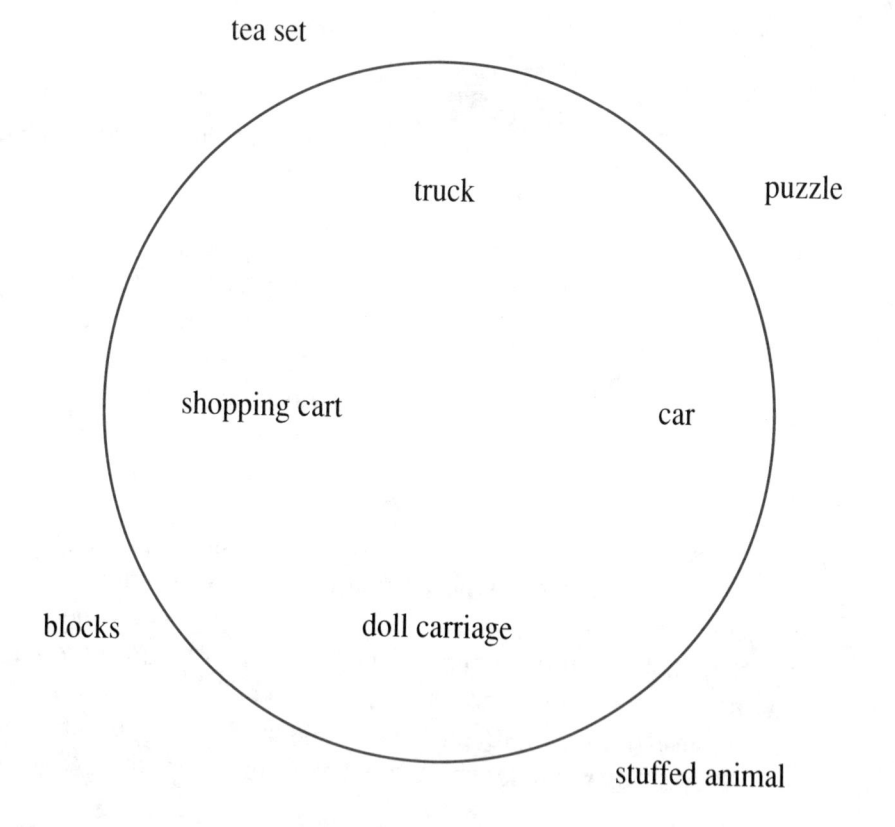

tea set

truck   puzzle

shopping cart   car

blocks   doll carriage

stuffed animal

Polar bears live in the Arctic.

They have white fur.

They have black eyes.

They like to eat fish.

Grizzly bears live in the woods.

They have brown fur.

5. Students may make up "What's My Rule?" sets of their own about books, science, animals, different cultures, and so on.

Newspaper Estimates

1. Use the newspaper to help students practice estimation in conjunction with reading and writing skills. Begin by asking each child to bring in an article from a local newspaper about something that interests him or her.

2. After each child has shared the subject matter of the article with the class, ask him or her to estimate how many times a particular word or type of word appears in the article. For example, you may ask a child to guess how many consonant-vowel-consonant ("cvc") words appear in the article (such as "dog," "cat," "bad," "sad," and so on).

3. After each student has written down a guess, have him or her go through the article and highlight the words that fall into the particular category. See how close their guesses were to the actual counts.

4. If desired, ask students to draw illustrations about their newspaper articles. Attach the illustrations and articles to a bulletin board under the title "Noteworthy News."

Name _____

Map-Making Mania

It's up to you to bury a treasure chest on Golden Island. Where should you hide it? Choose a hiding place, then write directions to tell someone where the treasure is located. The first step has been done for you.

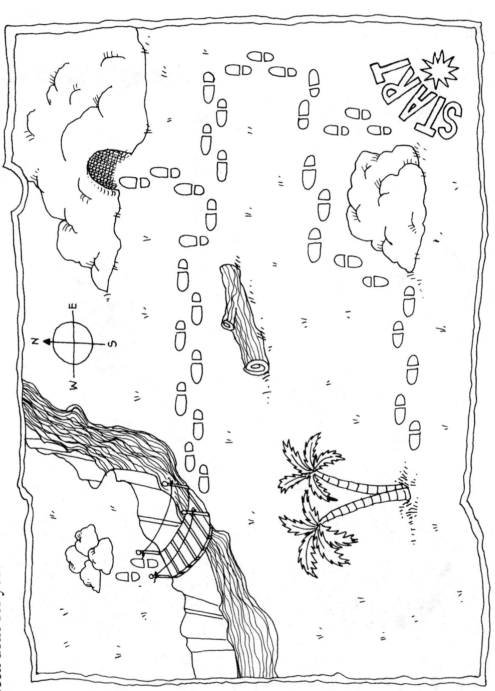

Go three steps north. _____

_____

_____

Now see if a friend can find where the buried treasure is located!

Serial Order
∙ ∙ ∙ ∙ ∙ ∙ ∙ ∙

Follow the directions below to put each set in serial order.

1. Draw the bears in order from smallest to largest.

2. Draw the blocks in order from longest to shortest.

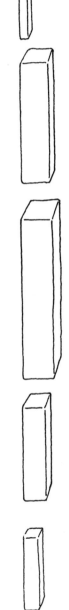

3. Draw the bowls of ice cream in order from fewest scoops to most scoops.

4. Now make up a serial order of your own. Write down the rule for your serial order.

Math Storybooks

Materials:

- 9" x 12" construction paper
- crayons or markers
- scissors
- stapler

Directions:

1. Ask students to choose one or more of the sets of figures on page 63 to use to make a math storybook. Reproduce the selected figures enough times to make several sets for each child.

2. Help children think of mathematical story lines that involve their selected figures. For example, if a student has selected the birds, he or she may write, "Once upon a time there were five birds who lived in a nest. One morning two of the birds decided to go out to play. Then there were three birds left in the nest...." After each student is satisfied with his or her concept, have him or her write out a draft of the story.

3. Distribute 9" x 12" construction paper to the class. Have students write their stories, and color and cut out their figures to use as illustrations.

4. Ask children to title their stories and make covers for their books. Staple the pages together in order. Encourage students to share their math storybooks with the rest of the class. Then place the books in the reading or math center for classmates to review during free time.

Math Storybooks

Answers

page 38 (clockwise)

1001	242	939	6556	535
+2002	+111	-717	+2222	-202
3003	353	222	8778	333

Answers for the second part of this exercise will vary.

page 39

```
    A5
  B1  6  3  2
    6
  C1  3   D6  8  9  E3
  F7  0  7  0      1
    2          G7  H4  2
  I9  0  J5      6
    0          6
  K3  6  0  L1      4
    1
    1
```

page 42

8 books; 4 stuffed animals; 4 shoes; 7 cassette tapes; 11 cars and trucks

1. There are four more books than stuffed animals.
2. There are more cassette tapes.
3. The total is 15.
4. There is the same amount of stuffed animals and shoes.
5. There are seven more cars and trucks than shoes.

page 44

Answers will vary. Possible answers include: One candy bar and five gumballs; 25 gumballs; six lollipops and two chocolate drops; ten peppermint sticks; one candy bar and two peppermint sticks; one candy bar and one chocolate drop; three lollipops, one peppermint stick, one chocolate drop, and one licorice; two licorices and five gumballs.

page 45

Answers will vary.

page 49

1. 41°F   5°C
2. 50°F   10°C
3. 58°F   14°C
4. 36°F   2°C

page 50

4	2	6
6	4	2
2	6	4

8	1	6
3	5	7
4	9	2

10	5	9
7	8	9
7	11	6

page 52

2 1/4 c. flour
1 c. sugar
1/2 c. brown sugar
1 tsp. baking soda
1/2 tsp. salt
1 c. butter
2 eggs
1 tsp. vanilla
2 1/2 c. chocolate chips
3/4 c. walnuts

page 60

Answers will vary.

page 61